AIR

© 1992 Franklin Watts

Franklin Watts, Inc.
95 Madison Avenue
New York, NY 10016

Library of Congress Cataloging-in-Publication Data

Richardson, Joy.
    Air/by Joy Richardson.
        p.   cm. — (Picture science)
    Includes index.
    Summary: Examines air, atmosphere, and clouds and how they are
affected by pollution
    ISBN 0-531-14201-9
    1. Air—Juvenile literature. 2. Atmosphere—Juvenile literature.
3. Clouds—Juvenile literature. 4. Air—Pollution—Juvenile
literature. [1. Air. 2. Atmosphere. 3. Clouds. 4. Air—
Pollution.] I. Title. II. Series.
QC161.2.R53   1992
551.5—dc20   91-42612
                                                    CIP AC

Editor: Sarah Ridley
Designer: Janet Watson
Illustrator: Linda Costello

Photographs: Christian Bonnington Library 23; Eye Ubiquitous 10;
Chris Fairclough Colour Library 28; Chris Fairclough/Franklin Watts 14;
Sally and Richard Greenhill 7; Robert Harding Picture Library cover,
title page, 13, 16, 20, 25 (inset); Frank Lane Picture Library 9, 19; ZEFA
25, 26.

Printed in Singapore

PICTURE SCIENCE

AIR

Joy Richardson

FRANKLIN WATTS
New York • London • Toronto • Sydney

Head in the air

There is air all around you.
Every few seconds,
you breathe some in through
your nose or your mouth.

The air goes into your lungs.
Oxygen from the air passes
into your blood and
around your body.

The oxygen helps to turn
the food you eat into energy.
Energy keeps you going.

You cannot live without breathing.

Breathing

Every living thing needs air.

Horses and hamsters,
cats and dogs all have lungs.

Worms take in air through their skin.
Insects breathe through
holes in their sides.

Fish take in air from the water
through gills in the
sides of their heads.

All animals need air
to keep them alive.

Green leaves

Plants need air, too.
They take in air through
tiny holes in their leaves.

Green leaves use part of the air,
called carbon dioxide, to help
make food.

Plants help to keep the air healthy.
When they make food,
they make oxygen, too,
and let it out into the air.

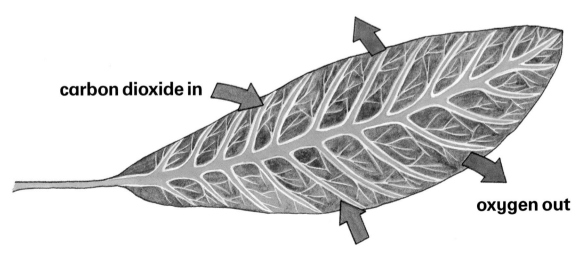

carbon dioxide in

oxygen out

11

Air against us

The air presses down on us.
We do not notice it
because we are used to it.

When we run, we have to
push against the air.

Cars are shaped to stop
the air from slowing
them down too much.

Parachutes use the
air as a brake
to slow themselves down.

Wind

The air does not stay still.
Warm air rises and
cool air rushes in
to take its place.

These air movements make
the winds that blow
the clouds across the sky.

The wind blows leaves around.
It carries seeds
from place to place.

The air can be very powerful.
Strong winds can blow trees down
and push trucks over.

Using the air

When you pump up a tire
or blow up a balloon,
the air is squashed in
until there is no room left.

Squashed up air can be
used to drive machinery.

Hot air is lighter than cold air.
This makes hot-air balloons
rise high into the sky.

Birds

Birds are built for flying.

They have light hollow bones
and well-shaped bodies that
cut smoothly through the air.

Birds push themselves through
the air with their wings
and steer with their tails.

They fan out their wings
like parachutes to slow
themselves down as they land.

Airplanes

Airplanes carry people
into the air so that they
can fly from place to place.

Airplanes have bodies and wings
that are shaped
to help the air lift them up.

Airplanes are big and heavy.
They need powerful engines
to push them along.

Jet engines take in air
that is squashed up and heated.
The air rushes out of the back,
like air from a balloon,
and pushes the airplane forward.

Climbing high

As you climb higher,
the air becomes thinner
and more spread out.

On high mountains,
climbers may need
extra oxygen supplies.

In high places there is
less air pressing down.
This can make people feel sick.

Airplanes are sealed to keep
the air pressure inside
feeling normal.

Dirty air

The air is precious and
we need to take care of it.

When anything burns it makes
smoke that hangs in the air
and is not good to breathe.

Cars, fires, and factories
can all make the air dirty.

When fuel burns, it lets off
carbon dioxide into the air.
This may alter the atmosphere.

The atmosphere

The air around the earth
makes up the atmosphere.

Birds, clouds, and airplanes stay
in the lowest layers
of the atmosphere.

Higher up, the air in the
ozone layer blocks out
harmful rays from the sun.

A hundred miles up,
satellites orbit the earth.
There is almost no air
to slow them down.

The atmosphere gradually
fades into space, where
there is no air at all.

Invisible air

You can see the air
if you take the lid off
an empty jar under water
and watch the air bubbling up.

You can squash the air
by blowing as much as
you can into a paper bag.

You can watch air resistance
at work if you drop a piece of paper.

Index